The Seven First Words of Christ

Jim Somerville

© 2020
Published in the United States by Nurturing Faith Inc., Macon GA,
www.nurturingfaith.net.

Nurturing Faith is the book publishing arm of Good Faith Media (goodfaithmedia.org).

Library of Congress Cataloging-in-Publication Data is available.

ISBN: 978-1-63528-094-4

All rights reserved. Printed in the United States of America.

Scripture quotations are from New Revised Standard Version Bible, copyright © 1989 National Council of the Churches of Christ in the United States of America. Used by permission. All rights reserved worldwide.

To the Members and Friends of
Richmond's First Baptist Church:

You inspire me.

Contents

Introduction 1
The First Word: Let It Be 5
The Second Word: Believe 15
The Third Word: Follow Me 25
The Fourth Word: Come Out 35
The Fifth Word: I Came 45
The Sixth Word: Be Clean 55
The Seventh Word: Say Nothing 65
Conclusion 75
About the Author 77

Introduction

Perhaps you have been to one of those Good Friday services that focused on the seven *last* words of Christ, with seven different preachers taking as their texts what Jesus said from the cross: three sayings from Luke, three from John, and one that is shared by both Matthew and Mark. I've been to those services. I appreciate them. But I've also noticed that the Jesus in Luke's Gospel, for example, is a good bit different from the Jesus in Matthew. One says, "Father, into your hands I commend my spirit." The other says, "My God, my God! Why have you forsaken me?" It's a reminder that the Gospels are different and that each evangelist is telling his own story of Jesus, in his own way, for his own reasons.

When I saw that most of the Gospel readings for Epiphany, Year B, were from the first chapter of Mark, I wondered if I could put together a sermon series on the seven *first* words of Christ in that particular Gospel. I asked myself: What would happen if we looked at the opening chapter of this earliest Gospel and let Mark tell the story of Jesus in his way? Of the many things Jesus said in his life, which would Mark want to include in his Gospel, especially at the outset? If what Mortimer Adler says is true, that the most important parts of any book are the beginning and the end,[1] then what would happen if we paid attention not only to the seven last words of Christ but also the seven first?

So I went through Mark 1 with a fine-toothed comb, and what I found was some words and some deeds, but in the end seven distinct episodes from that action-packed chapter: 1) Jesus is baptized; 2) he begins to preach, 3) calls some disciples, 4) teaches in the synagogue, 5) heals the sick, 6) defines his mission, and 7) cures a leper. In order to include Transfiguration Sunday, I combined 5 and 6 and added the Transfiguration story from

Mark 9, but in the end the series came together so well that I've decided to share it in this little book. I've had to do some pushing and pulling to package the lectionary readings for Epiphany, Year B, as the "Seven First Words of Christ," but I don't think I've done violence to the text. My hope is that by the end of it you will not only have a fuller appreciation of Mark 1, but also a brighter and clearer picture of the Christ he wants us to know.

Finally, this may be a good place to express my gratitude to Bill and Elizabeth Childrey, who provided the funds to turn this idea into a book. May their generosity be rewarded by a deeper knowledge of the Christ who inspired these pages.

—*Jim Somerville*

Note

[1] Mortimer J. Adler, *How to Read a Book* (New York: Touchstone, 1972), pp. 32-35.

The First Word:
Let It Be

Mark 1:4–11

Mark doesn't tell us anything about the birth of Jesus. He doesn't waste his time on angels and shepherds, wise men and camels. His Gospel comes out of the starting gate as if there were no time to lose:

> This is the beginning of the good news about Jesus, the Messiah, the Son of God! As it is written in the prophet Isaiah, "See, I am sending my messenger before you, who will prepare your way; the voice of one crying out in the wilderness, 'Prepare the way of the Lord, make his paths straight!'"

And that's when Mark tells us about John the Baptist, who appeared in the wilderness, preaching a baptism of repentance for the forgiveness of sins. Mark says that people from the whole Judean countryside and all the people of Jerusalem were going out to him and were baptized by him in the Jordan River, but you have to wonder why, don't you? I can't imagine that if someone were hosting a festival of repentance at a downtown convention center the whole city would show up for it. But that's not all it was. It wasn't only about repentance; it was about repentance as a way of getting ready for the One who was to come, and these people wanted to be ready for that.

It had been 400 years since the voice of a prophet had been heard in Israel, and centuries since there had been any hint at all that God still cared about his people. As the nation was occupied by first one foreign government and then another, the people pleaded with God to send someone who would deliver them from their enemies and bring Israel back to its former glory. So when John the Baptist came onto the scene, looking very much like the prophet Elijah and talking about the One who was to come, the people got excited. Mark says,

> John was clothed with camel's hair, with a leather belt around his waist, and he ate locusts and wild honey. He proclaimed, "The One who is more powerful than I is coming after me; I am not worthy to stoop down and untie the thong of his sandals. I have baptized you with water; but he will baptize you with the Holy Spirit."

So if repentance and baptism were what it took to get ready for his coming, they would do it.

Then Jesus came to be baptized, and that presented a problem.

It doesn't present a problem for Mark, apparently. In his version of this story, he simply says that "Jesus came from Nazareth of Galilee and was baptized by John in the Jordan" (v. 9). But it presents a problem for Matthew, and for many of us as well, because John's baptism was a baptism of repentance for the forgiveness of sins and we believe Jesus was sinless. We get this idea from passages like 1 Peter 2:22 ("He committed no sin, and no deceit was found in his mouth"), from 1 John 3:5 ("and in him was no sin"), and from Hebrews 4:15 ("For we do not have a high priest who is unable to sympathize with our weaknesses, but we have one who has been tempted in every way, just as we are—yet was without sin").

So we might wonder why a sinless Jesus would come for a baptism of repentance for the forgiveness of sins if he had nothing to repent from and no sins to forgive. In Matthew's Gospel, John tried to prevent him, saying, "I need to be baptized by you, and do you come to me?" But Jesus answered him, "Let it be so now, for it is proper for us in this way to fulfill all righteousness." These are the first words out of Jesus' mouth in the Gospel of Matthew, and if we could borrow them for our study of Mark 1, I think we might benefit from trying to understand what Jesus meant.

How does the baptism of a sinless man "fulfill all righteousness"? I could almost understand it if Jesus had said it after he predicted his death on a cross, when Peter protested and said, "God forbid, Lord, this shall never happen to you!" I could almost understand it if Jesus had said, "Let it be, Peter," because it almost makes sense that the sacrifice of a sinless man would save us from our sins. But what does the *baptism* of a sinless man do for us or for him? Why was Jesus baptized? He said it was to "fulfill all righteousness," and for years I have suggested that his answer may only be another way of saying, "It's the right thing to do."

But that suggestion only raises another question: If baptism is, for Jesus, the right thing to do, why is it the right thing? So I dug a little deeper and discovered that the word Jesus uses here for *righteousness* is the same word Paul uses so often in the book of Romans—*dikaiosune*. It is an important word for Paul. When he talks about the righteousness of God, he means not only God's perfection and holiness; he means God's ability to make *us* right. *Dikaiosune* is the "right-making" power of a righteous God. It's what he uses to forgive our sins, straighten us out, and bring us back into right relationship with him.

It's what the father did when the prodigal son came limping home, looking like a wreck. He ran down the road to meet him, threw his arms around his neck, brought him back to the house, filled the tub with warm water, laid out some clean clothes, killed the fatted calf, hired a four-piece band, put shoes on the boy's feet, a ring on his finger, and threw a party to end all parties because his son who was lost had been found; the one who had been as good as dead was alive again.

Now that's power, and it's God's kind of power. When Jesus at his baptism says to John, "Let it be so now, for it is proper in this way for us to fulfill all righteousness," he uses that same word—*dikaiosune*—which makes me think Jesus's baptism is one part of the process by which a righteous God makes us right. The whole process is described by Paul in Philippians 2:5–11, where he says,

> Christ, though he was in the form of God, did not count equality with God as something to be exploited, but emptied himself, taking the form of a slave, being born in human likeness, and being found in human form he humbled himself, and became obedient to the point of death, even death on a cross. Therefore God also highly exalted him and gave him the name that is above every name, so that at the name of Jesus every knee should bend, in heaven and on earth and under the earth, and every tongue should confess that Jesus Christ is Lord, to the glory of God the Father.

Do you see how the line of movement in that passage goes down and then back up again, how Christ shrugs off his glory and descends lower, lower, and lower, until he is at last in the grave, and then how God lifts him higher, higher, and higher, until every knee is bending and every tongue confessing that Jesus Christ is Lord? If Jesus is going to fulfill all righteousness, if he is going to be the one through whom God makes us right, then it isn't enough for him to be "like" us; he must become one of us, and I believe that's what he was doing in his baptism. Paul says he was "born in human likeness," "found in human form," but in his baptism "he humbled himself." He waded out into water that was still muddy with human sin; he allowed himself to be immersed in the human condition; he came up one of us because it is only as one of us that he can do any of us any good.

When I asked on my blog once why Jesus was baptized, a number of people came up with similar answers. Linda Moore, a hospital chaplain, said, "I wonder if Jesus's baptism was another way for Jesus to 'step into our sandals' if you will—allowing the opportunity to connect on a human level with Jesus that we would not otherwise be able to do." Retired missionary Paul Burkwall quoted Baptist scholar Frank Stagg, who said, "Jesus was baptized as a way of identifying with those sinners he had come to save." Robert Gray, a Sunday school teacher, quoted Baptist pastor Guy Sayles, who said, "In the experience of baptism…Jesus identified deeply with his people's sinfulness, taking it on himself." Finally, military chaplain J. T. Moger said Jesus was baptized "to show solidarity with, and to identify with, sinners." If all of that is true, if Jesus really was baptized to show his solidarity with sinful humanity, we still need to ask why. What was so important about becoming one with people like us?[1]

I remember, early in my ministry, standing on a front porch hearing confession. I had gone to visit a woman who had dropped out of church years before. She didn't invite me in, but as I stood there, she told me how she didn't think God could ever forgive her. She had done a lot of bad things, she said, but the worst of those was turning her back on God after the death of her mother.

I tried to comfort her. I told her we all make mistakes. I said, "I've made a lot of mistakes myself."

"Don't say that!" she snapped. "Don't tell me you've made mistakes. You're a preacher, and I put preachers up on a pedestal."

And then I wanted to tell her what she had told me: "Don't say that!" Because I know what every preacher knows—I am only human, and as a human I share with people everywhere the human tendency to make mistakes, to sin. I'm not proud of that, but I do know this: While it might be nice to be up on a pedestal, you can't do ministry from up there. You might be able to hand down judgment or blessing, but you can't sit by someone's hospital bed when you're on a pedestal; you can't hug someone who's hurting; you can't hear what someone confesses in a whispered voice.

Jesus knew this, so when John tried to put him up on a pedestal, when he told the crowds he wasn't worthy to untie the thong of Jesus's sandal, and when he told Jesus that he, John, should be baptized by him, Jesus said, "Let it be, John, for it is proper for us in this way to fulfill all righteousness." In other words this is the way God has chosen to use his remarkable right-making power—by coming down off the pedestal, being born as a helpless child, wading out into water still muddy with our sin, and allowing himself to be immersed in the human condition. Jesus was baptized with a bunch of sinners not because *he* was a sinner, but because he knew you can't do your best ministry from a pedestal. No one can.

Not even God.

I'm not sure John understood that. I think his head was probably still full of questions when he finally consented and dipped Jesus down under those muddy brown waters. But when he brought him back up again, the sky was torn open, and the Spirit came down, and a voice from heaven said to Jesus, "You are my Son, the beloved. In you I am well pleased!" which makes me think that even if John didn't get it, God did. He knew what it would take to make us right. It would take someone who was equal to God but not afraid to empty himself of his divinity, to come down off the pedestal, to be found in human form. It would take someone who wasn't ashamed to humble himself, to wade out into water still muddy with human sin and be baptized into the human condition. It would take someone, in other words, who knew that what we needed was not a God up there, somewhere, but one who was right down here where we are. That is to say that what we needed, more than any of us even knew…

…was Jesus.

Note

[1] These comments were made on blogpost http://www.jimsomerville.wordpress.com/2009/01/08/why-was-jesus-baptized.

The Second Word:
Believe

Mark 1:12–15

The Second Word: Believe

When Barack Obama was inaugurated in January 2009, it occurred to me that if Martin Luther King had still been around, he would have been eighty years old; if he were still able, he would have almost certainly been on the program; as he sat there on the platform, he might have been overcome by the significance of the occasion.

A little more than forty-five years earlier, King had gathered a crowd at the other end of the National Mall and told them he had a dream that someday people in this country would not be judged by the color of their skin but by the content of their character. In the same way the statue of Abraham Lincoln looked over Martin Luther King's shoulder on that day, the legacy of Martin Luther King was looking over Barack Obama's shoulder on inauguration day.

I feel certain Obama was aware of that legacy and that he felt the full weight of Dr. King's dream. Expectations had probably never been higher. And I considered how he must have given thought to the words he would speak after he was sworn in—his first words as president. After his election he must have tried out a hundred different lines, tested those words on his tongue, wondered if they were worthy of the moment or if they would live on beyond it. I understand that on that Saturday night, after his train rolled into Washington, he spent some additional time working on that speech. If it were you, you would want to be sure your words were just the right words for the occasion, and in the weeks between your election and your inauguration, you would think about that.

According to Mark, the time between Jesus's election and his inauguration was forty days. At his baptism the heavens were torn open, and the Holy Spirit came down, and the voice of God said, "You are my Son, the Beloved; with you I am well pleased." It was an election, if you will—a moment when Jesus was chosen to carry out the mission of the Messiah. Immediately after that (according to Mark), Jesus was driven into the wilderness by the Holy Spirit, where he was "tempted by Satan." Mark doesn't tell us what that temptation was like, but if we can trust Matthew and Luke (and I think we can), it was a time when Jesus had to do some deep thinking about who he was and what it meant to be the Son of God. "If you are the Son of God," Satan said, "then do this, or this, or this." And each time the devil tested him, Jesus proved that he was the Son of God by answering with the Word of God and doing just what his father would have wanted.

But think about it for a minute: forty days in the wilderness to consider what it would mean to be the beloved Son of God and what sort of shape his ministry should take. I've spent a little bit of time in the wilderness of Judea—the Negev Desert, just south of Jericho. It's beautiful in its own way, but there is almost nothing there except blue sky above and rocky, hilly ground below. My tour guide quoted a minister from one of her trips, who said it is no wonder the three great religions of the world were born in the desert: "There is nothing there except you and God" (except in Jesus' case, where the whispered voice of the tempter was his constant companion: "If you are the Son of God…if you are…if…"). And not only that, Mark says, but "he was with the wild animals," which I think was probably not—as one commentator suggested—a fulfillment of Isaiah 11, that peaceable kingdom where the lion lies down with the lamb and a little child shall lead them. As I said, I've spent some time in the wilderness, and I know how the slightest noise can wake you up at night and leave you staring into the darkness wondering what

The Second Word: Believe

made it. The Bible describes the wilderness as a place haunted by lions and jackals, and I can almost picture Jesus curled up in the soft dust under a rock overhang, using a smooth stone for a pillow and starting at every sound.

But it wasn't only wild animals who kept him company. Mark says that the angels "ministered to him," which reminds me of those ravens who fed Elijah when he was in the wilderness. Who knows what sort of food ravens would feed a prophet, but day after day they came, flapping in on those shiny black wings, clutching in their claws just enough to keep Elijah going. And even though Matthew and Luke say that Jesus fasted in the wilderness, Mark says the angels waited on him. You can almost picture them flapping in on their dazzling wings late in the afternoon when Jesus was squinting into the setting sun, bringing with them just what he needed to make it through long nights filled with animal noises and long days filled with the whispered voice of the Tempter.

Forty long days, actually, and I don't think we can even imagine how long that would seem if you were in the wilderness by yourself. My brother Ed once went up the mountain behind our house in West Virginia, telling us he was going to spend three days fasting and praying and trying to figure out what he was supposed to do with his life. He was ready to be done after the first few hours, but he stuck it out. It didn't hurt that he found an abandoned cabin up there where he could clear away some cobwebs and get out of the elements, especially on that second night when it rained so hard. He lay on an upper bunk thanking God for a dry place to sleep, but when he woke up the next morning and saw a four-foot-long copperhead curled up on the floor beside his bed—one of those wild animals who had also come in out of the rain—he wasn't nearly so grateful. He came down off the mountain finally with a notebook full of questions and only one real answer: that he should devote his life to God. These days Ed is a missionary in Mexico, where a little experience with spiders and snakes comes in handy.

I think about Jesus out there in the wilderness with all his questions: "What does it mean to be the Son of God? What shape should my mission take? What am I supposed to say?" But in the end it came down to one thing. After John had been arrested and thrown into prison, Jesus left Judea and entered Galilee. On the way, he preached the message that had come from all those days of wilderness wondering, the distillation of forty days in the desert. That long, thoughtful pause between election and inauguration had led to this urgent message:

1. The time is fulfilled,
2. The kingdom of God has come near.
3. Repent and believe the gospel.

For all the attention it received, the time between Martin Luther King's speech and Barack Obama's inauguration was nothing compared to the time God's people had been waiting for the fulfillment of his dream. And for all the majesty, all the dignity, of a dream in which people of different races can live together in harmony, it pales by comparison to God's dream of a time when every valley would be exalted and every mountain and hill made low, when the crooked places would be made straight and the rough places plain, and all flesh would see the salvation of our God. A dream not only of a peaceable kingdom, but of God's kingdom come to earth—that's the dream Jesus preached.

When I talk about the kingdom of God, people sometimes ask me what it is, and I answer simply that the kingdom of God is wherever God is king, and that could be anywhere. It could be in you, in your home, in your church, even in your city.

When I was teaching fifth- and sixth-grade Sunday school, I tried to make it even more concrete. One morning I took some masking tape and marked off a square on the carpet. I asked my students to imagine that inside that square, God was king. I asked them one at a time to step inside and tell me what it felt like in the kingdom. They said they really couldn't tell much difference from any other spot in the classroom, but they also acknowledged that if God really did rule over their lives day by day, their lives would be different. And as we talked, they seemed to think it might be a good thing, and that part of what God might want from them was to enlarge that kingdom, to make the masking tape square a little bigger until it took in the whole classroom, and then the church, and then the town where we lived.

That's what Jesus was talking about when he said the kingdom of God had come near. It wasn't here yet, but the time had at last been fulfilled, and the kingdom of God was waiting just outside the door. All that was needed for the kingdom to come was for God's people to get up out of their chairs and come to the door.

In Mark's Gospel, Jesus has authority over the forces of evil and the forces of nature. He can cast out demons and rebuke the devil; he can wither a fig tree and still the wind and waves. But he has no authority over the human heart. He can bring his kingdom to your front door; he can knock till his knuckles are bloody. But he cannot make you get out of your chair. And that's why he says, "Repent and believe the gospel."

He's begging.

The word he uses for "repent" is *metanoia*; it's a "head" word that means "to change your mind." If you thought the kingdom of God was coming in some other way, change your mind. If you thought it was going to come with the sound of warfare and roll of stirring drums, change your mind. If you thought it was going to come with the sound of a trumpet and stars falling from the sky, change your mind. If you thought it was going to come with God's voice thundering in your ears, demanding your life, change your mind. The kingdom comes with a gentle knock and waits for your response. So do it. Respond. Get up out of your chair. Open the door.

Let it in.

And then Jesus said, "Believe in the good news." The word he uses for "believe" is *pisteuo*; it's a "heart" word, and it involves getting down off the throne in the throne room of your own heart and letting God sit there instead. What he says goes, so he really does become the king of your life. There, at least, the kingdom really does come.

We Christians believe that one day the Jesus who came will come again. When he does, it will not be with a knock on the door and a whispered invitation, but with power and great glory. On that day he will not say "repent"; he will not say "believe"; he will not say "the kingdom has come near"; he will say the kingdom is here and now, and woe to the one who waits until that day to make a decision. For all the excitement about what happened in Washington on the day of Barack Obama's inauguration, for all the talk about how the time had been fulfilled and King's dream had finally come true, I want you to recognize that something far more significant could happen right here, right now. As you are reading this book, you could decide that the time has come to step down off the throne of your life and let God sit there instead. This is just the way it happens—not on the front page of the newspapers, not on CNN. The kingdom of God comes secretly, quietly—one human heart at a time.

The Third Word:
Follow Me

Mark 1:14–20

The Third Word: Follow Me

When I was a pastor in North Carolina, I also served as an adjunct professor on the faculty of Wingate University. Three mornings a week for most of the time I was there, I would walk from my office at the church to a classroom on the campus, where I would try to teach religion to college freshman at nine o'clock in the morning. One of my regular offerings was a course called "Jesus and the Gospels," and on that first day of class—after I had gone over the syllabus and answered any questions—I would give my students their first homework assignment, which was to read through the Gospel of Mark in one sitting.

"Make sure you have good light and a comfortable chair," I would say. "Don't forget to go to the bathroom first. And then sit down and read through the whole Gospel as if you were reading a very short novel. It should take about an hour." I don't know how many of them actually did it, but when they came to class next time, I assumed that they had, and I would ask them about their impressions of the Gospel.

Many of them were impressed by how quickly the Gospel moves: "Immediately," Mark says, "Jesus went from here, to here, to here." Some were impressed by how impatient Jesus was with his disciples and how dense they seemed to be. And someone would always ask why Jesus cursed that poor, fruitless fig tree in chapter 11.

Reading the Gospel in one sitting gives you a different feel for it than hearing a few verses at a time in a worship service. You come away with an overall impression of the Gospel—and probably an image of Jesus that is not as gentle, meek, or mild as you once imagined. He seems to be in a hurry in this Gospel, anxious to get somewhere or accomplish something and impatient with those dim-witted disciples who couldn't seem to keep up. He turned over tables in the temple, and on at least one occasion, yes, he took out his frustration on a fig tree and withered it to the roots. Not all of my students were churchgoers, and some of them would ask about Jesus, "Who is this guy? And what does he want anyway?" "Aha!" I would say. "That's just what we're going to talk about…next time."

At the beginning of that next class period, I would pull out a copy of an article that I've had for years. It's by a writer named Genni Gunn, and it's called "Getting Your Novel Started in Ten Days."[1] I found it when I was thinking about writing a novel, and I've kept it because I sometimes still think about it. But I've also kept it because it helps me understand the Gospel of Mark. "Okay," I would say to my class, "let's change the name of the article slightly. Let's call it, 'Getting Your Gospel Started in Ten Days.' And let's imagine that Mark is reading it as he sits there at his desk getting ready to write."

Day 1," Ms. Gunn suggests: "Define your idea. Begin by asking yourself, 'What *is* my Gospel about?' Write a one-sentence summary." "Hmm," Mark says. "What is my Gospel about? It's the good news about Jesus, the Messiah, the Son of God" (and by the way, if you look up Mark 1:1, you'll see that's exactly the sentence he wrote down. And then, I imagine, he took the rest of the day off).

Day 2," Ms. Gunn continues: "List your characters." "Not so hard," Mark says, chewing the end of his pencil. "There's Jesus, and Peter, and the other disciples, and all the people he healed, and the scribes and the Pharisees, and Pilate, and, and…. That ought to be enough for one day."

Day 3," Ms. Gunn continues: "List locations and settings." "Oh, that's not so hard either," Mark says, taking out a clean sheet of paper. "There's the Jordan River, and the Sea of Galilee, and all those little towns around it, and then, of course, Jerusalem, the garden of Gethsemane, Golgotha...." And then he chokes on the memory and can't bring himself to write anything else.

"Day 4," Ms. Gunn suggests, cheerfully: "Define your characters' goals. Your main characters must want something they are unable to get. In one sentence, define what each of your main characters wants." And this is usually where I would turn away from Mark, sitting at his desk, and turn to my students, sitting at theirs. "In this Gospel," I would ask, "what does Jesus want that he is unable to get?" And then I would watch them struggle, those earnest young men and women, many of whom had grown up going to Sunday school in Baptist churches, wrestling with the idea that Jesus, the Son of Almighty God, might want something he couldn't get. And then light would break across the face of one of my brighter students, and she would raise her hand, tentatively, and I would say, "Yes? Do you know what Jesus wants that he can't get in this Gospel?" "I think so," she would say, gulping. "I think he wants to establish the kingdom of God." "Exactly!" I would say, slapping the desk, making the whole class jump. "That's exactly right! Jesus wants to establish the kingdom of God on earth as it is in heaven, but he can't do it because we won't let him."

Again, if you read the Gospels carefully, you will find that Jesus talks about the kingdom more than any other thing. One hundred twenty times, mostly in the first three Gospels, he refers to the kingdom or its equivalent. If I had asked you at the beginning of the sermon to define the word *gospel*, you might have said that the gospel is the good news of how Jesus came to save sinners, or the gospel is the good news that God cares for the poor. In Mark's Gospel, Jesus doesn't say all that much about saving sinners. He gives passing notice to the poor. The *main* thing he talks about is the kingdom of God. From the beginning of the Gospel to the end, you can see that he is trying to get that project off the ground. So when my students came back to class, we spent some time talking about the kingdom of God and what it meant to Jesus.

"A kingdom," I would say, reading right out of the dictionary, "is a territory, people, state, or realm ruled by a king or a queen. It is any place or area of concern thought of as a sovereign domain. In other words, a kingdom is wherever the king is in charge. The kingdom of God, then, would be wherever God is in charge. That could be a nation, or a city, or a household, or a human being. I think Jesus would say that if God is in charge of your life, then the kingdom of God is in you!" And that's usually where I had to stop talking about the kingdom, because there is only so much you can say in a classroom, even a classroom at a Baptist university. You have to maintain a clear distinction between instruction and indoctrination. But in the church it's different. In the church you don't have to hold back.

You see, when we talk about the kingdom of God in church, we remember that there was a time when God *was* king. When Joshua brought God's people into the promised land, he challenged them to choose whom they would serve, and they said they would serve the Lord. He would be their God; he would be their king; they wouldn't need anybody else but him. But then they got into trouble with some of their hostile neighbors and God raised up heroes for them—"judges," they were called—who helped them defeat their enemies and restore the peace, people like Gideon and Deborah and Samson.

But soon the judges weren't enough. The people wanted more. They wanted a king like other nations, and eventually—in spite of Samuel's protests—they made Saul their king. What they didn't seem to understand is that before they could put Saul up on the throne, they had to drag God down. And that's just what they did. In one of the most poignant moments in Scripture, God tells Samuel, "Look, they're not rejecting you; they're rejecting me."

So when Mark picks up his pen to write, he writes to an Israel that has suffered the corruption and loss of its earthly kingdom, an Israel that has been carried off into exile in Babylon, an Israel that has spent the last 400 years trying to recover. He writes a story about a young prince who has come to reclaim his father's lost kingdom, and that's where our Gospel reading for today picks up, right at the beginning of the adventure. Jesus, the beloved Son of God, freshly baptized and full of conviction after forty days' testing in the wilderness, begins to make his way up the road from Judea to Galilee, alongside the river and around the shore of the lake, preaching to every person he meets along the way: "The time is fulfilled, and the kingdom of God has come near; repent, and believe in the good news."

But here's the catch: Although it is his father's lost kingdom Jesus has come to reclaim, it's not a claim he can force. Jesus has authority over the forces of evil and the forces of nature: He can cast out demons and calm the wind and the waves. But Jesus has no authority over the human heart, and in that sense it is true that Jesus—the hero of this Gospel—wants something he cannot get. He wants to plant the flag of his Father's kingdom in the life of every person he encounters, but he can only do so with every person's permission. He can only do so with your permission.

And if you know anything at all about yourself, you know what a hard job it will be—because we love being in charge of our own lives. We love sitting on the throne, and wearing the crown, and waving the scepter. In short, we love being king, and to let someone else take over is hard for us. We lay down the scepter reluctantly. We grudgingly give up the crown. We slide off the throne feeling wretched and miserable—how will we ever adjust?

What Jesus has to convince us of is the truth about his Father: that his Father loves us and knows us better than we know ourselves. He has to convince us that if we will ever yield the throne, we will find ourselves in the care of one who can bring forth more from our little lives than we could have ever dreamed or imagined. Our dreams for ourselves are too often small and self-serving. God's dreams for us are always large and other-serving—world-serving. If we could ever give ourselves up to those dreams, give ourselves over to that God, then I think his kingdom would come, and his will would be done, on earth as it is in heaven. But just try taking a scepter out of someone's hand. Just try prying the crown off his head. You'll find out in a second what a big job it is, and I think Jesus figured that out before he got halfway around the Sea of Galilee.

Mark tells us that when Jesus called Peter and Andrew, James and John, they left their nets and followed him, but what Mark doesn't tell us is how many people Jesus called before he got to those four. It may have been dozens, hundreds. There were lots of little fishing villages along the shores of Galilee in Jesus's time and at least one large city. He may have said to everyone he met, "Follow me," but until he got to Capernaum, until he got to these first disciples, no one did. I thought about that in a staff meeting recently. There had been hundreds of people in worship on the Sunday before, and thousands more watching on television, but the person we were talking about that day was a girl named Jasmine, who had responded to the invitation at the end of the service and come down the aisle to tell me she wanted to follow Jesus. There may have been others who were *this close* to coming down the aisle, but she was the one who came, and hers was the story we were telling.

In the same way there might have been dozens, even hundreds, of people who were *this close* to responding when Jesus told them the time was fulfilled, the kingdom of God had come near, maybe thousands who were on the verge of getting down off their thrones and following when he begged them to repent and believe the gospel. But the ones we hear about are the ones who actually did it: Peter and Andrew, James and John. They left their nets and followed, even though they must have had little idea of who he was and less idea of where he was going. It takes a lot of faith to do that. It takes a lot of courage.

And so we come to the end of this chapter. If it were a sermon and we were in a worship service, I might extend to you the same invitation Jesus extended to those first disciples. If he were saying it himself, he would say it this simply, this directly: "Follow me." And then he would wait for your response. It is a simple invitation, but it is not an easy one. Jesus is asking you to give up control of your own life and hand it over to him, to step down off the throne of your own life and let him sit there instead. He is asking you to fall in behind him and trust him with your future. It is no wonder that so many people refuse that invitation. The wonder, really, is that anyone accepts it at all.

Note
[1] Genni Gunn, "Getting Your Novel Started in Ten Days" *The Writer's Handbook*, Sylvia K. Burack, ed. (Boston: The Writer, Inc., 1990), pp. 134-135.

The Fourth Word:
Come Out!

Mark 1:21–28

The Fourth Word: Come Out!

When Jesus was just getting started in his ministry, he went to the synagogue in a little fishing village called Capernaum, where they were good enough to let him preach. They were glad they did, because he was like no other preacher they had ever heard. He didn't spend all his time quoting from the commentaries or telling them what other people had said about the Bible; he just told it like it was, and what it was, was good. You got the feeling, when he said something, that it was God's own truth and not just his or anybody else's opinion. When he finished, they looked at each other and said, "Have you ever heard anything like that? This man preaches with *authority*, and not like our scribes. They're always talking about how things were; he tells it like it is!"

But while they were still bragging on him, the door of the place banged open, and in came a man possessed by an unclean spirit. His eyes were wild! His whole was body twitching. There were flecks of foam around his mouth. He came right up to the front of the synagogue and pointed at Jesus, shouting, "What business do you have here with us, Jesus? You Nazarene! I know what you're up to. You're the holy one of God, and you've come to destroy us!" But Jesus wouldn't have it. "Quiet!" he said, like a man calling down a dog. "Get out of him!" And the man went into spasms, his arms and legs jerking violently, his eyes rolling back in his head. And then, with a sudden surprised gasp, as if he had just been punched in the stomach, he crumpled to the floor and lay there like a dead man.

You could have heard a prayer shawl drop.

And then a woman came out of the crowd, pushed her way forward, and dropped to her knees beside him. She cradled his head in her lap, wiped the foam from his mouth with the hem of her skirt. "Samuel?" she whispered. "Samuel?" His eyes fluttered open, and he looked up at her as if she were vaguely familiar, as if he had met her somewhere years before. And then his eyes went wide with recognition. "Mother?" he said. "Mother?!" And she sobbed and hugged him to her bosom as the room began to buzz with curiosity. "What is this?" the people wondered. "A new teaching, with authority. He commands even the unclean spirits, and they obey him!"

When I was just beginning my ministry, I went to a church in a little town called New Castle, Kentucky, where they were good enough to let me preach. On my first visit the search committee showed me a pictorial directory, and I pointed to a picture on the first page. "Who's this?" I asked. "Oh," they said, embarrassed, "you don't have to worry about her. She doesn't come anymore." But then they went on to tell me the story about this woman, how she had been diagnosed as paranoid schizophrenic, how she used to carry a gun in her purse when she came to church. You can imagine how surprised I was when I stepped up into the pulpit on my first Sunday as pastor and saw that woman sitting on the second pew with a great big purse on her lap. Several times as I was preaching, she thrust a hand down into that purse, and each time I imagined the headlines in the next day's newspaper: "Baptist minister shot dead during first sermon. Woman claims she 'didn't care for his exegesis.'" But she didn't shoot me dead, and after that first nerve-wracking encounter, I got to know, and came to love, Helen.

She *was* paranoid. She would call me from time to time cussing and fuming and claiming that someone had been in her apartment and stolen everything she had. When I would go down there to see what she was talking about, she would show me. "See?" she would say, as if it were obvious to everyone. "This stack of towels used to be right here. Somebody has moved it over here! And this jar full of pennies? It used to be right here on the front of my dresser. Somebody has shoved it all the way to the back!" You couldn't argue with her about these things. You just had to listen and nod. If it was real to her, it was real. But then the phone calls started coming more and more frequently until I had to propose a radical solution. "If you would just give your things away," I said with a smile, "you wouldn't have to worry about anyone stealing them." Christy and I got a good bit of Tupperware that way, a collection of steak knives, and a full set of stainless-steel flatware with the letter "A" on the handle—the first letter of Helen's last name. We used that flatware for years, and when people asked me why it had an "A" on the handle instead of an "S," I just smiled and said, "We're collecting the whole alphabet."

Truth be told, there were plenty of people at New Castle Baptist Church who wished that Helen would just go away again. She would get up during the worship services to take her medication, and that was okay; everybody wanted her to take her medication. But she would wander down to the front of the church when she did it, stopping sometimes to rearrange the flowers on the communion table before going out the side door to the water fountain. It was a little distracting for all of us. And then there was the singing. Helen loved to sing, but her voice was loud and harsh and toneless, and when she sang, it sounded like someone yelling hymns through a bullhorn. One member of the choir got particularly upset about that and finally announced, "I'm just going to tell her not to come back. She's loud, and she's crazy, and she can't sing. We'd all be better off if she'd just go away." And I said, "Be careful. Be careful. There's a person in there."

I knew some things about Helen that the choir member didn't know. I remembered, for example, the night she had called me to ask if I would take her to the slightly bigger town down the road to get a refill on her prescription. It was a cold, rainy night. The town was thirty miles away on a twisty two-lane road. I didn't want to go. But she said she needed her medicine, and I knew just how much she needed it. So I put on my coat, got in the car, and went to her apartment. Helen was in a foul mood, angry and complaining all the way there, telling me how mean her neighbors had been and all the things they had done.

When we got back in the car to head home, I decided to change the subject. "Let's sing," I said, and started right into "Amazing Grace." It took her a while to get into it, but eventually she did, singing right along with me in that screeching voice of hers. We sang "The Old Rugged Cross" and "Power in the Blood" and "Shall We Gather at the River." And then she looked over at me and asked, "Do you know that song 'When I Take My Vacation in Heaven'?" I didn't, so she sang it for me, the whole thing. And then she asked, "Do you know that song 'Will I Shake My Mother's Hand in Heaven'?" I swallowed hard and said no, and then she sang that one for me too. When she got out of the car, she was all smiles, and she thanked me for the best evening she'd had in a long time.

It was not long after that that she gave me the handwritten manuscript of a book she was working on. It was called "A Life without Love," and it chronicled the abuse she had received as a child, the divorce of her parents, the death of her mother. It was just about the saddest thing I had ever read, and it made me think that if I had been through what she had been through, I might be paranoid too. She told me once that her favorite psalm was Psalm 31: "I am the scorn of all my adversaries, a horror to my neighbors, an object of dread to all my acquaintances; those who see me in the street flee from me. I have passed out of mind like one who is dead; I have become like a broken vessel. For I hear the whispering of many—terror all around!—as they scheme together against me, as they plot to take my life" (vv. 11–13).

Whatever else he may have been, the man with the unclean spirit who came into the synagogue in Capernaum that day was someone like that: the scorn of all his adversaries, an object of dread to his acquaintances, someone from whom everyone flees. But Jesus was able to see immediately that it wasn't the man himself who was the problem; it was that unclean spirit inside him. If you could get that out, the man would be fine. This is one of the things I love most about Jesus: that he sees the person before the problem. Where we say, "He's a thief," Jesus might say, "He's a child of God." Where we say, "She's an alcoholic," Jesus might say, "She's a human being." Where we say, "He's a sex offender," Jesus might say, "He is no less precious to God." It's not that Jesus excuses our bad behavior; it's just that no matter how badly we twist and bend God's intentions for our lives, Jesus knows who we are.

So when the man with the unclean spirit came charging into the synagogue in Capernaum, Jesus saw him for what he was: a man. And he saw the problem for what it was: an unclean spirit. He didn't confuse the man with the spirit any more than a dentist confuses a man with a bad tooth. "This thing's got to come out!" the dentist says. But that's not what we say, is it?

We put the two together. We wring our hands and say, "This man is an alcoholic. Isn't that a shame?" instead of saying, "Quick! Alcohol is trying to kill this man! We've got to do something!" Jesus saw what this unclean spirit was doing to the man, but he also saw what needed to happen: that spirit needed to come out. He wasn't confused about it for a moment, didn't spend any time trying to reason with the man—he spoke directly to the spirit. And in language stronger than he would have used with any human being, he said, "Shut up and come out!" And the spirit came out. The people were amazed. "What is this?" they said. "A new teaching, with authority! He commands even the unclean spirits, and they obey him."

I've told you before that the Greek word for "authority" is *exousia*. It means "out of the substance." In Jesus' case his authority came out of his own substance. He wasn't like those scribes who were always quoting some respected rabbi. He just said what he meant and meant what he said. And when it came to casting out unclean spirits, he didn't need to consult the manual. He just said, "Be quiet and come out." Because, as one of the old creeds affirms, the substance of which he was made was the substance of God himself, and when he spoke, he spoke with God's own authority. He could see that man in the synagogue for all God had made him to be, and he could also cast out of him everything that kept him from being that man.

He can still do that.

I don't always tell this story, but once Helen called me at church just after worship. She was furious about something, ranting and raving and yelling into the phone. I decided I would go down the hill to see her, but I didn't want to go alone, so I asked one of my deacons—Roger—to go with me. When we got to Helen's apartment, she was storming from room to room, screaming about all the things that had been stolen from her and the dastardly wretches who had done it. Roger and I listened carefully, but as she pointed out examples of how this had been moved to there and that had been moved to here, we realized this was just one more of her paranoid episodes. I finally asked if I could pray with her, thinking it might calm her down, but she didn't want me to pray for her. She wanted me to find the people who had done this and bring them to justice, to call the police, to call her lawyer! But at last she fell into a chair, exhausted, and I put my hand on her shoulder and began to pray. I didn't know what to say. I just asked the Lord to do for her what I couldn't—to give her peace of mind. As I prayed, I felt her body relaxing under my hand, and when I said "Amen," she looked up with a sweet smile and thanked me for coming as if I had just stopped by for a glass of iced tea.

We went out and got in the car, and Roger, who had grown up in the Pentecostal tradition, asked me if I had seen what he had. "What was that?" I asked. "While you were praying for her," he said, "I saw a big snake come out from under her chair and go out the door. Didn't you see it?"

"No," I said. "I had my eyes closed."

To this day I don't know what Roger saw, or if he actually saw anything. He had quite an imagination. But I do know that when we invite Jesus into the room, incredible things happen. We hear things we have never heard before. We see things we have never seen. And like that congregation in Capernaum we are often left speechless, astounded, amazed. "What is this?" we say. "A new teaching, with authority. He commands even the unclean spirits, and they obey him."

The Fifth Word:
I Came

Mark 1:29–39

THE FIFTH WORD: I CAME

You may not believe it, but those of us in the preaching profession sometimes wonder if it does any good. We work at our sermons week after week, study the scriptures, consult our commentaries; we jot down notes on paper napkins, practice dramatic gestures, think out loud; when Sunday comes, we stand in the pulpit with pounding hearts, say our piece, and then step down for the closing hymn, wondering if it has made any difference at all.

I was at my first church for almost five years. Those were good people in that small Kentucky town. They were honest, hardworking, kind. But were they any better at the end of my tenure? Had my preaching made any difference? I don't know. I was at my next church twice as long. Those people, too, were fine Christians when I came and fine Christians when I left. But were they any finer? Had my preaching done anything for them? I'm not sure it had. The same could be said for my church in Washington. Did my preaching leave any lasting impression on those people? Were they formed in any way by my many words? It's hard to say.

When a man digs a ditch, at the end of the day he knows just how much of the ditch he has dug. But when a man preaches a sermon, he can't really tell how much of his work has been done and how much is left to do. I'm not trying to make you feel sorry for me; I'm only saying it because it's true. I work with words, not spades, and the digging I do is not the kind that can be easily seen. It is measured in fractions of inches, not feet. If preaching has any results at all, they are often inner and invisible, and that's why ministers are often tempted to spend their time on other, more measurable things.

I got a call from a former seminary classmate once who told me he was going into full-time evangelism. "How did you make that decision?" I asked, and he talked about being in Russia when Billy Graham was there, about having the opportunity to preach once himself and seeing people respond by the hundreds to his invitation. I could understand the appeal of that kind of ministry. How satisfying it would be to say, at the end of a week, "A hundred more souls saved. Guess I can take tomorrow off!"

Ministers often get involved in building programs before they really need to so they can see some results from their labor, so they can point back at the end of their tenure and say, "At least there's that." Others spend time in counseling or visiting, both of which can be more rewarding than the time it takes to prepare a thoughtful sermon. Preaching is like cooking, and the lasting benefits of serving a meal and delivering a sermon are roughly the same. At least, that's how it seems.

At one of my churches I knew a man who was confined to a wheelchair. He was a university professor, just about my age, and the interesting thing about his story is that he hadn't always been in a wheelchair. One afternoon when he was a teenager, he played basketball with his brother. When he woke up the next morning, he couldn't feel his legs. From that morning to this one, he has not been able to walk.

That kind of tragedy can make you bitter, or it can make you better. In Greg's case it made him better. He began to focus his energies on his studies, exploring his love for mathematics and eventually producing a 600-page doctoral dissertation. After his father's death Greg was a great comfort to his mother. Somehow, in his care for her and her care for him, she made it through her grief. She told me once about Greg, "He's the best person I know." He is the best person a lot of people know. He is patient, and thoughtful, and funny, and wise. He is loved by the people of that little town, by his students at the university, and by the members of his church family. It was one of those—a member of his church family—who once asked me what I would do if I were Jesus.

"If I were Jesus?"

"Yeah. What would you do?"

"Hmm...I guess I would try to do the things Jesus did. I mean, I'm not sure I could improve on that. How about you?"

He was quiet for a moment, thoughtful, and then he said, "I would heal Greg."

And then we were both quiet, imagining Greg getting up out of that chair, standing straight and tall, taking his first steps in more than thirty years. If my friend were Jesus, that's what he would do, which raised for both of us the following question: Why didn't Jesus do it?

In this book I've been writing about the seven first words of Christ in the Gospel of Mark. Even though Mark doesn't record them here, some of those words were words of healing. After he cast out that unclean spirit in the synagogue, Jesus came to Simon Peter's house and found Peter's mother-in-law in bed with a high fever. He took her by the hand and lifted her up. Immediately, the fever left her, and she began to wait on them. News of the healing got out the door somehow. By sundown, when the Sabbath officially ended, Jesus had plenty of work to do. Mark says "the whole city" was gathered around the door.

Tell me the truth: If you knew there was someone in your town who could heal the sick, or even if you only thought he might be able to heal the sick, isn't there someone you would want to bring to him? Isn't there some wheelchair somewhere you would want to roll up to his door? Some hospital bed you would want to push through the city streets? Maybe you would want to bring yourself, under your own power, for the healing you alone know you need. Can you imagine standing before him as he looks into your eyes and asks, "What do you need me to do for you, daughter? What kind of healing do you want, my son?" Whatever their reasons, everybody in the little town of Capernaum found some reason to be outside the door where Jesus was in the hope that he could heal. And he did heal. He worked late into the night apparently, "curing many who were sick with various diseases and casting out demons." He was a sensation, and the sensation created a crisis in his ministry.

Mark tells us that Jesus was tempted by Satan in the wilderness, but he doesn't give us many details. You have to look to Matthew or Luke for that. There we learn that Satan tempted him first of all by asking him to turn stones into bread. It would have been a good thing to do. There were so many stones out there in the wilderness that if anyone could turn them into bread, that person could feed the nation, the world. And that would be a good thing, wouldn't it? Behind Satan's suggestion that Jesus turn stones into bread to feed his own hunger was the more subtle temptation to feed the world's hunger, and Jesus must have labored over his answer. "Man does not live by bread alone," he said at last, "but by every word that comes from the mouth of God." It was a recognition of the difference between those things that are temporal and those that are eternal. Feed someone today and you will have to feed him again tomorrow, but give him the word of life and he can live forever.

Does that mean we have no obligation to feed the hungry? Of course it doesn't. In the church I serve, we collect food week after week. We store it on shelves in our food pantry. We put it in

The Fifth Word: I Came

bags and give it to those who need it. As long as there are hungry people in the world, the followers of Jesus will have an obligation to feed them, as he did when the multitudes were hungry. But both he and we know there is a difference between that which fills the belly and that which feeds the soul. One lasts for a few hours; the other can last forever.

But think back to that evening in Capernaum when Jesus was touching and healing the sick. Think of the wonder on their faces, the gratitude, as crippled limbs were straightened, as atrophied muscles grew strong, as people walked who hadn't walked in years, as they leaped and danced and whirled. Think of those who were doubled over with illness standing straight and tall, those who were covered with weeping sores becoming clean and whole, those who were dying of disease feeling healthy and strong again. Could there be anything on earth more satisfying than having that power and using it for that purpose? The gratitude would have been overwhelming, the response enormous. News would have spread like wildfire through the hills of Galilee, and every person who could push a wheelchair would be pushing one—fast—to that place where Jesus was.

These are the thoughts that must have been going through his head as he tried to sleep that night. Exhausted by the day's events he would have fallen into bed sometime after midnight and dropped off immediately, but after a few hours, after the strength had come back into his body, he would have started to stir, would have seen their faces again, the desperate need that was there—the hands reaching out toward him, trying to touch him; the mothers holding their babies; the fathers carrying their sons. He would have tossed and turned on his narrow bed, reliving the whole experience until sometime long before daybreak he got up and slipped out the door to find a quiet place to pray.

He went to the "wilderness," Mark says, a word that has only been used once before in this Gospel. The wilderness is where the Spirit drove him to be tempted by Satan. On that morning in Capernaum, it seemed to be driving him again to a place where he could wrestle with temptation. The temptation that faced him in that hour was the temptation to make his ministry a ministry of healing alone. It was such an obvious need, and people were so obviously grateful for it. He could spend the rest of his days healing and never run out of opportunity, never run out of appreciation. But praying in that deserted place early in the morning, Jesus must have come to the painful realization that all healing is temporary. We get well only to get sick again. We stand up only to fall down. In the end these mortal bodies of ours must surrender to their mortality, and even if we had been healed by Jesus fifty times in our hundred years, we would still die. It was that thought that must have come to his clouded mind in the sobering act of prayer. And when the disciples came looking for him, he was ready.

"Where have you been?" they asked. "We've been searching for you everywhere. Everyone wants to know where you are." In their minds they may have already decided what course his ministry should take. They would open a clinic right there in Capernaum; put up a nice big building with a large, comfortable waiting room. They would pave a few acres for a parking lot and put up a sign over the door that read, "Real miracles, sensibly priced."[1]

"Let's go," they said. "Everybody is looking for you."

But Jesus surprised them with his answer: "Let's go to the other towns in the area so that I can preach the gospel there too. That's what I came to do." In the discipline of prayer, Jesus had wrestled with temptation and redefined his mission. He hadn't come to heal the sick, but to establish God's kingdom, and the best way to do that—he believed—was not through healing but through preaching.

So Sunday after Sunday, I step up to the pulpit, believing along with Jesus that it makes a difference—not that sudden, dramatic difference that everybody is talking about the next day, but that almost imperceptible difference that works in a person's life like yeast working in a lump of dough until, over time, it makes all the difference in the world. William Willimon says about preaching, "Sometimes a word is heard. Someone is challenged all the way to the tip of the soul; the world is torn apart and reconstructed in such a way that that person can only turn around and be converted or else live embarrassingly out of step with the way he or she clearly sees the world to be."[2]

That's what we hope for, we preachers, and that's why we keep preaching. We're hoping that through the foolishness of what we preach, a word might be heard, a life might be changed, and the kingdom of God might come at last, on earth as it is in heaven.

Notes

[1] Steve Martin. *Leap of Faith*. Film. Directed by Richard Pearce. Irving, Texas: Paramount, 1992.

[2] William H. Willimon, *What's Right with the Church* (San Francisco: Harper & Row, 1985), pp. 111-112.

The Sixth Word:
Be Clean

Mark 1:40–45

THE SIXTH WORD: BE CLEAN

There used to be a billboard along Highway 74 in North Carolina that showed a photograph of a woman who had been badly beaten, lying in a hospital bed. I can still see it in my mind's eye—her eyes were black, her cheeks were bruised, her lips were split and bleeding. It was part of a campaign to end spouse abuse in that county, and its intent was to provoke an emotional response in those people who passed by.

It worked.

The first time I saw that billboard, two equally strong emotions welled up within me: One was pity for this horribly abused wife; the other was rage for the husband who had done it to her.

Is it possible to feel both rage and pity in the same soul at the same time? If so, is it possible Jesus sometimes felt that way too?

In this episode from Mark 1, Jesus is approached by a leper who says, "If you choose, you can make me clean." Most of the ancient manuscripts—most of them—say at this point that Jesus was "moved with pity," but a few of them—and only a few—say he was "filled with rage."

Rage? *Really?*

Is it possible he felt both, as I did when I saw that billboard? Did he feel pity for the victim and rage for the perpetrator? Well, yes, I suppose it is possible. But who "perpetrates" leprosy? Who's to blame? Was Jesus angry with God, as we sometimes are when we don't know who else to be angry with? Was he angry at the person who "gave" the leper this contagious disease? Or was he angry with the whole situation, with the whole infuriating chain of events that could turn a healthy human being into the pitiful creature now kneeling at his feet? Because there must have been a time when the leper was not a leper at all.

We can't really reconstruct the story of his life, but from the detailed descriptions and prescriptions in Leviticus 13, we can get an idea of what happened to him. There it says that "when a person has on the skin of his body a swelling or an eruption or a spot, and it turns into a leprous disease on the skin of his body, he shall be brought to Aaron the priest or to one of his sons the priests" (13:2).

It could have been that simple. A boy could have come home from school, or from doing his chores, or from playing with his friends on the Galilean hillsides. His mother could have fed him supper and listened to the story of his day. And that night, while she was washing behind his ears, she could have noticed a spot or a swelling.

"What's this?" she would ask.

"I don't know."

"How long have you had it?"

"I don't know."

She would have watched it for a few days, but when it only seemed to be getting worse, she would have bundled the boy up as you would to visit the doctor and hauled him off to see the local priest.

"The priest shall examine the disease on the skin of his body," says the book of Leviticus, "and if the hair in the diseased area has turned white and the disease appears to be deeper than the skin of the body, it is a leprous disease; after the priest has examined him he shall pronounce him ceremonially unclean" (13:3).

"Hmmm," the priest would say, examining the boy at arm's length, covering his mouth and nose with his prayer shawl. "This looks bad. This looks very bad." And then, straightening himself, he would drop the shawl and look at the boy's mother with sad eyes, knowing what his next words would mean: "This boy has leprosy," he would say. "He is unclean." And then, according to the law, there would be only one thing left to do.

"The person who has the leprous disease shall wear torn clothes," says the book of Leviticus, "and let the hair of his head be disheveled; and he shall cover his upper lip and cry out, 'Unclean, unclean.' He shall remain unclean as long as he has the disease; he is unclean. He shall live alone; his dwelling shall be outside the camp" (13:45–46). And so it would be that this boy—who had been an ordinary boy, with friends and family and maybe even a dog—would become a leper, living in the hut his father would make for him outside the village, eating the food his mother would bring each day, but other than that cut off from the world of the living, cut off from the life he had enjoyed.

A leper.

To be fair to the book of Leviticus, those laws had been given to keep the whole village from becoming a leper colony. Leprosy was understood to be a highly contagious disease, requiring the quarantine of those who had it in order to keep it from spreading to everyone else. The problem is not with the book of Leviticus but with what happens to human beings when you give them the authority to pronounce some things clean and other things unclean. They become fascinated with the difference. They draw finer and finer lines. They make more and more laws.

In a book called *Meeting Jesus Again for the First Time*, New Testament scholar Marcus Borg writes that by the time of Jesus, the religious leaders of Israel had become obsessed with the idea of cleanliness.[1] They had as their guiding principle the words of Leviticus 19:2: "You shall be holy, for I, the LORD your God, am holy." Holiness, they believed, was God's defining attribute, and for them holiness was separation from anything that was unholy, anything that was unclean. So while your mother might have said, "Cleanliness is next to godliness," the religious leaders of Israel might have said, "Cleanliness *is* godliness."

But what is clean? What is unclean? And who gets to decide? The answer? The religious leaders! And in centuries of making such distinctions, they had come up with an elaborate "purity code" to distinguish between those who were "in" and those who were "out" as far as God was concerned. According to Borg those who were "in" were typically pure, righteous, healthy, rich, Jewish, and male. Those who were "out" were impure, unrighteous, diseased, poor, Gentile, female, or any combination of the above.2 Not surprisingly, those who were most "pure" were those who were most like the religious leaders themselves, and those who were least "pure" were those who were least like them. Do you see how it makes a difference who gets to make the rules?

But before we start condemning the religious leaders of ancient Israel, we need to recognize how much we are like them. We have come up with our own purity codes, our own ways of determining who is clean and who is unclean. For example, until a few years ago the race for president of the United States had always come down to a contest between two white, educated, affluent men. It was a strong statement about who we judged to be "clean" and "unclean" in this country. For more than 200 years, as Americans cast their votes for such people, they cast them against the non-white, uneducated, poor, and female citizens of our nation.

But before we start condemning public opinion, take a look around you at church. If we have gathered in the name of the one who loves the little children, "red and yellow, black and white," why are so many of us only white? Why are so many of us educated? Why are so many of us affluent? There are exceptions to the rule, of course—people who are brave enough and self-confident enough to go to church wherever the Spirit leads them—but most of us tend to go where feel most comfortable, and we tend to be most comfortable with people who are just like us. Although we are not always conscious of it, we have come up with our own purity code, and although we may not be able to articulate it, most of us know the difference between the kind of person who would be a "good prospect" for our church and the kind of person who would not.

If Jesus did become "filled with rage," as a few of the old manuscripts attest, it was because of this: Those who considered themselves righteous had drawn a circle around themselves and pronounced everyone inside the circle clean and everyone outside the circle unclean, including the leper who knelt at Jesus's feet. And if Jesus was moved with pity, as most of the old manuscripts affirm, it was because the leper said to him, with tears leaking from his eyes, "If you choose, you can make me clean." Did you hear that? He didn't say, "You can make me well." He didn't say, "You can make me whole." He said, "You can make me clean," because in his time and culture the difference between being in and being out was the difference between being clean and unclean. And Jesus said, in a voice filled with emotion, "I do choose. Be made clean!" Breaking through the manmade barrier between purity and impurity, Jesus touched the untouchable; "immediately," Mark says, "the leprosy left him, and he was made clean."

I believe it was right there, in that moment, that Jesus came up with his own code—not a code of purity, but a code of compassion. In Luke 6:36, in language so similar to Leviticus 19:2 as to be an intentional substitute for it, Jesus says, "Be compassionate, as God is compassionate." God's defining attribute is not his purity, but his compassion—his ability to "feel with" those who are suffering and do something about it—and that God's people should share that attribute above all others.

When I was a pastor in North Carolina, some of us used to go out to a nearby trailer park on Saturday afternoons to work with the children who lived there. They were the poorest of the poor in that little town, and I thought it was just the kind of place where Jesus would spend his time. There was a woman in our group named Debbie who was short and round. By the time she had huffed and puffed her way up the hill to the trailer where we did our ministry, she would have to sit down. In summer I would bring a chair outside for her, and she would sit there in the yard as we rounded up the children.

There was one little girl, Neecie, who would always come running to Debbie. Neecie was the dirtiest child in the trailer park. None of the other kids would play with her, and you wondered if there was anyone at all who cared about her. Her hair was always wildly out of place. She had stains on her clothes, grape jelly smeared on her cheeks. She smelled of human sweat and chicken grease and dirty diapers. A priest would have pronounced her "unclean."

But Debbie didn't.

Every Saturday afternoon Neecie would come running straight to Debbie and beg to be lifted up into her lap. I would watch as Debbie took a deep breath, swallowed hard, and then bent down to scoop Neecie up into her arms. But then something beautiful happened. Neecie would settle onto Debbie's lap, relax into her embrace, and let out a sigh of perfect contentment. And then she would always look up at Debbie and say with a smile, "You soft!" (which really is the highest compliment you can pay to a lap).

Let that image stay in your mind like a billboard beside the highway. Let it fill you with rage that such scenes are so rare in our world. Let it fill you with pity for that little girl and all the others like her. Finally, let your eye fall on the caption printed at the bottom of the picture and remain there until the words have been engraved on your heart: "Be compassionate, as God is compassionate."

Notes

[1] Marcus Borg, *Meeting Jesus Again for the First Time: The Historical Jesus & the Heart of Contemporary Faith* (San Francisco: HarperCollins, 1994), 50ff.

[2] Ibid., 52.

The Seventh Word: Say Nothing

Mark 9:2–9

The Seventh Word: Say Nothing

I once preached an Epiphany sermon in which I talked about it as the "feast of lights" and joked about how I wanted to flood the sanctuary with light so the congregation would have to feel its way out of the room at the end of the service, temporarily blinded, and how someone strolling along the street in front of the church might see all that and say to his wife, "Look, Ethel. Must be Epiphany." But if the truth be told, there wasn't much light at that first Epiphany—just a single star shining over that house in Bethlehem, just enough light for the wise men to look on the face of a little boy and see him for who he really was, and fall down and worship him.

But apparently they were the only ones who saw him for who he really was. In Matthew's Gospel there are no angel announcements, no heavenly choirs, no shepherds racing through the streets to share the good news. There is no recognition that a savior has been born, really, apart from that extraordinary visit from the wise men, and even that doesn't come until Jesus is nearly two years old. It is only much later, after he has been baptized, when he begins to preach and teach and heal, that people begin to figure out there is something special about this man. And then it is like dialing up a dimmer switch on the wall: With everything he says, with everything he does, the light gets a little brighter; Jesus' identity becomes a little clearer until we come to this moment on the mount of transfiguration, when he is bathed in light so dazzling that the disciples have to shield their eyes.

That's what I've been trying to do in this book: As I have focused on "the seven first words of Christ," I have tried to reveal a little more about him in each chapter, tried to turn the dimmer switch up brighter and brighter, so that by this point you could see him for who he really is.

1. The first word is "Let it be," and I wrote about Jesus' baptism as a way of immersing himself in the human condition, of becoming one with us so we could hear his message. "Let it be," he told John, "in order to fulfill all righteousness."
2. The second word is "Believe," and I wrote about the kingdom of God and Jesus's insistence that the kingdom can be a reality for anyone who will come down off the throne of their lives and let God be king. "Repent and believe this good news!" Jesus said.
3. The third word is "Follow me," and I wrote about how Jesus had authority over the forces of nature and the forces of evil, but no authority over the human heart, how he might have called hundreds of people before those first disciples followed, how he calls each of us and waits to see if we will come.
4. The fourth word is "Come out," and I wrote about how Jesus cast out an unclean spirit and how he always seemed to maintain a distinction between the person and the problem. I told the story of Helen, my paranoid parishioner, and mentioned how I always tried to remember there was a person in there.
5. The fifth word is "I came," and I wrote about how Jesus was tempted to make his ministry a ministry of healing alone but in the end decided that if the kingdom was going to come, it would come through preaching, not healing, and bringing in the kingdom was the reason he had come.

The Seventh Word: Say Nothing

6. The sixth word is "Be clean," and I wrote about how, for Jesus, compassion was even more important than purity, how he demonstrated that compassion by touching and cleansing a leper, bringing him back into the community even though it violated the terms of the "purity code."

With every word I've tried to dial the dimmer switch up a little more, reveal a little more about Jesus, so you can see him for who he really is, which makes this chapter's word a bit unusual: "Say nothing."

You may remember it from the end of the Gospel reading in the last chapter. After Jesus had cleansed the leper, he sent him away, sternly warning him to say nothing to anyone but to go and show himself to the priest so he could be pronounced clean. But this man went out and began to proclaim it freely, Mark says, "so that Jesus could no longer go into a town openly, but stayed out in the country; and people came to him from every quarter" (1:45). With every word he said, with every deed he did, Jesus revealed a little more about himself, and as it became clear that he was someone with the power to cleanse and heal, it became impossible for him to move about freely. He had just told his disciples he wanted to go to the other cities of Galilee to preach the gospel, but now he can't go anywhere without drawing a crowd. This is why he told the former leper to say nothing to anyone. But I think there was another reason too.

Let me just ask you to remember why Jesus came. Did he come to heal the sick primarily? No. If he had, he would have stayed in Capernaum. Did he come to cleanse the lepers primarily? No. If he had, he would have sent the leper to round up all his friends. In Mark's Gospel at least, Jesus seems to have come to establish the kingdom of God on earth as it is in heaven, and the way he is going to do that is through preaching, teaching, and training his disciples to take over the work when he is no longer around. Because that time will surely come. If you keep asking people to step down off the throne of their lives and let God sit there instead, eventually you will meet up with some resistance. If you keep asking people to give up their power, eventually those people who have power, even if it's only a little bit, will find a way to shut you up.

In the very next chapter of Mark's Gospel, four friends bring a paralyzed man to Jesus and let him down through the roof. Jesus tells the man, "Son, your sins are forgiven," and some of the scribes who are sitting there begin to accuse Jesus of blasphemy, of claiming to do something that only God can do. A few paragraphs later, the scribes of the Pharisees complain that Jesus is eating with tax collectors and sinners, a violation of their purity code. A few paragraphs after that, Jesus' disciples pluck a few heads of grain from a wheat field, and the Pharisees accuse them of breaking the Sabbath law. In the next chapter Jesus heals a man with a withered hand; immediately, Mark says, "the Pharisees went out and conspired with the Herodians against him, how to destroy him" (3:6). Do you hear that? It's only chapter three, and already the religious authorities are trying to figure out how to kill Jesus! It's not because he is healing people; it's because he has power, and his power threatens their power, and they don't want to give theirs up. So they have to find a way to stop this man permanently.

This is why he told the leper to say nothing to anyone—because he is trying to bring in the kingdom, and if the leper goes blabbing all over the countryside, then Jesus won't be able to move about freely. Almost from the beginning of the Gospel, the religious authorities are looking for a way to trap Jesus, to keep him quiet, to limit his power, to put an end to him. And almost from the beginning Jesus is looking for a way to ensure the success of his mission even if he is not there to carry it out. He preaches constantly about the kingdom. He calls and trains some disciples. He tells those he heals to keep quiet. But with everything he says and with everything he does, he is revealed a little more clearly for who he really is.

Part of that is intentional, I think. He wants his disciples to know who he is. If they are going to carry out his mission, they will have to believe that they are on a mission from God, not man. In chapter eight of Mark's Gospel, Jesus asks his disciples what they are hearing about him, who people are saying he is. "Some say you are John the Baptist, come back from the dead," they say. "Some say you are Elijah, or one of the other prophets." "What about you?" Jesus asks. "Who do you say that I am?" "You are the Messiah," Peter says, and then Jesus sternly ordered them not to tell anyone about him. It was just after that that he began to teach them that the Son of Man must undergo great suffering; and be rejected by the elders, the chief priests, and the scribes; and be killed, and after three days rise again.

Do you see how the two are connected? That when the disciples finally figure out Jesus's secret identity (and only then), he can tell them what's going to happen next? It's like he doesn't want the religious authorities to find out because they will try to stop him, but he wants the disciples to find out because they will need to carry on. And so in public he is always pressing a finger to his lips, telling people to keep quiet, but in private he is sharing with his disciples the secrets of the kingdom, training them to carry on his work.

Which brings us at last to this moment on the mountain, when Jesus is alone with Peter and James and John. Mark says that he was transfigured before them and that his clothes became dazzling white, whiter than any bleach on earth could make them. And suddenly Moses and Elijah were standing there with him, talking to him, and Peter blurted out, "Rabbi, it's a good thing we're here. Let us put up three little huts: one for you and one for Moses and one for Elijah!" He didn't know what to say; he was scared out of his wits. But that's when the cloud settled on top of the mountain and a voice from the cloud thundered, "This is my son, the beloved. Listen to him!" And suddenly Moses and Elijah were gone, and the cloud was gone, and they were left alone with Jesus. On the way down the mountain, he told them to say nothing to anyone about what they had seen, until after the Son of Man had risen from the dead.

Why all this secrecy? Why couldn't the disciples run down the mountain shouting, "Jesus is the beloved Son of God!"? Because the moment they did it, the religious authorities would have nailed Jesus to a tree. That's how threatened they were by his power. That's how much they wanted to hold on to their own. And if they had done that then and there, the disciples would have been left to carry on without him, trying to establish God's kingdom before they had been fully trained. They needed that image of Jesus on the mountain, with Moses on one side and Elijah on the other. They needed to hear God say about him, "This is my beloved son." Those words and those images would sustain them in the days ahead, when things got difficult. But they needed even more than that. They needed to see Jesus ride into the city of Jerusalem on a donkey. They needed to hear the crowds welcome him as king. They needed to watch him confront the religious authorities. They needed to hear his warnings of the days to come. They needed to sit with him at the last supper. They needed to share his body and blood. Only then would they be ready to let him go. Only then would they be ready to carry on.

It's remarkable, really. The more Jesus was revealed for who he really was, the more the religious authorities wanted to cover it up. The more his light shined in the world, the more they wanted to snuff it out. So it's remarkable that the disciples were able to learn enough about him to carry that light forward. It took effort on his part. He had to keep shushing the crowds, and whispering to his disciples, and sharing the secrets of the kingdom, but in the end it worked. His enemies tried to shut him up, snuff him out, but his friends couldn't keep quiet. They kept telling everybody about this Jesus, about all the things he had said and all the things he had done. And they never forgot what happened on the mountain that day. In one of his letters Peter says,

> For we did not follow cleverly devised myths when we made known to you the power and coming of our Lord Jesus Christ, but we had been eyewitnesses of his majesty. For he received honor and glory from God the Father when that voice was conveyed to him by the Majestic Glory, saying, "This is my Son, my Beloved, with whom I am well pleased." We ourselves heard this voice come from heaven, while we were with him on the holy mountain. (2 Pet 1:16–18)

Why is it that we, who have become convinced that Jesus is the Messiah, the Son of God, his beloved boy, so often say nothing at all about him? The time for secrecy is past, friends. Jesus has risen from the dead.

It's time to go public.

Conclusion

In the end, what we have is Mark's picture of Jesus, set apart from those of the other evangelists. For Mark, Jesus is both the long-awaited Messiah and the Son of God, but a son who immerses himself so fully in the human condition that he becomes one with us. He strides forth out of the wilderness, proclaiming the good news that the time is fulfilled and the kingdom of God is at hand, and then he calls disciples who will help him bring in the kingdom.

He still does.

He exercises his authority over the forces of nature and the forces of evil, but not over people. Instead, he invites them to let God have his way in their lives, to let him be king until his kingdom comes on earth as it is in heaven. In this kingdom everyone matters—the sick, the blind, the lame, the lepers, the demon-possessed, you and me. There was a time to keep quiet about the coming kingdom, but that time is past. Now that Jesus has passed the work on to us, it's time to get busy, time to spread the news.

It's time to bring in the kingdom.

—*Jim Somerville*

About the Author

The Rev. Dr. James Green Somerville is pastor of the First Baptist Church of Richmond, Virginia. He is only the sixteenth senior pastor since the church was founded in 1780. A gifted preacher and a seasoned pastor, he has preached on the Chicago-based "30 Good Minutes," the internationally broadcast Day1 radio program, and was one of the featured preachers at the Festival of Homiletics at the Washington National Cathedral in 2004. His articles and sermons have been published in *Christian Century, Leadership, The Upper Room, Preaching, Lectionary Homiletics,* and *Preaching Great Texts.* He was awarded the Clyde T. Francisco Preaching Award while a student at the Southern Baptist Theological Seminary in Louisville, Kentucky.

Jim served as pastor of the First Baptist Church of the City of Washington, DC, for seven years before coming to Richmond. Prior to that, Jim served as pastor of Wingate Baptist Church in Wingate, North Carolina, for nine years. While attending seminary, Jim was pastor of First Baptist Church in New Castle, Kentucky.